NATIONAL GEOGRAPHIC

Spiders

PATHFINDER EDITION

By Beth Geiger

CONTENTS

Jumping spider

Spiders
Weaving Wonders

Spiders don't win many hearts. Yet these eight-legged hunters are awesome animals. Earth wouldn't be the same without them.

By Beth Geiger

How would you like living with 50,000 spiders? Chuck Kristensen loves it. He thinks spiders are cool. Big hairy tarantulas, crawling brown recluses, and lots of other spiders share Kristensen's home. He sells spider venom, or poison, to scientists. They use the venom to make medicines.

Cute as a Spider?

Is Kristensen nuts? Everyone knows spiders are scary, harmful, and gross—right? Well, not really.

Yes, spiders can be dangerous. A bite can leave a painful bump on your skin. And some spiders are poisonous. Yet most are shy and seldom bite humans.

"Spiders have gotten a bad rap," says Kristensen. Spiders are actually fascinating, important animals. They live on every continent except Antarctica.

There are at least 37,000 species, or kinds, of spiders. They come in many shapes, sizes, and colors. Some are as small as a pencil point. Others are as big as a bowl.

Spiders can even be cute. Honestly! What could be more adorable than a little jumping spider, gazing at you sweetly with its dark eyes—all eight of them?

Body Basics

Spiders may bug you, but they aren't insects. They're **arachnids** (uh RAK nidz). Spiders' cousins include scorpions and ticks.

Along with eight legs, a spider has two main body parts. One is its head. The other is a back section called the **abdomen** (AB duh mun). The whole spider is covered with hair. The hairs help a spider sense nearby objects.

Two stubby limbs stick out from the head. Spiders use them like hands. Spiders also have jaws that end in sharp fangs. Each fang has a tiny hole that releases **venom**.

The abdomen contains organs that help spiders do something special—make silk.

Silk Factories

Spider silk begins as a fluid. It oozes out from the spider's abdomen. Air turns the fluid into tough fiber. In fact, spider silk is stronger than steel.

Spiders use their silk to do lots of things. They tie up **prey**. They also make draglines. Those are threads that act like safety ropes. They keep a spider from falling.

Females wrap silk around their eggs to protect them until they hatch. Some spiders even make silk "parachutes" to sail off into the sky and find new homes.

Then there's the best known use of spider silk—making webs.

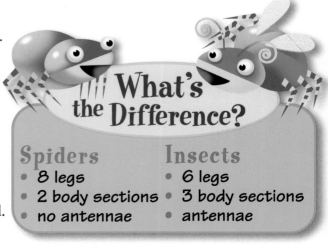

What's the Difference?

Spiders
- 8 legs
- 2 body sections
- no antennae

Insects
- 6 legs
- 3 body sections
- antennae

Mighty King.
Africa's king baboon spider (above) is a fierce hunter. It eats scorpions, frogs, reptiles, young birds, and other creatures.

Web Wizard. The orb weaver (above) makes familiar round webs. E.B. White's beloved Charlotte was an orb weaver.

Stamping Out Prey. *That stamp-size net (above) could be the last thing a cockroach or an ant sees. Net-casting spiders wait for prey to come close. When one does, the spider tosses the net to catch it.*

Color Change. *Some crab spiders (above) can turn yellow or white. Changing color can help a spider hide from predators or prey by making it look like part of a flower.*

Wide World of Webs

Spiders weave many kinds of webs. But they always use their webs to catch prey.

Some spiders make orb webs. That's the kind that looks like a wheel with spokes. Building one takes at least an hour. The result is a work of art.

Once the web is done, the spider waits in the middle. The instant an insect flies into the sticky threads, the spider jumps into action. It races over and injects the prey with venom to paralyze or kill it.

Purseweb spiders do things differently. They live inside tube-shaped webs. When an insect strolls by, the spider bites it, chomping right through the silk. The spider then drags the victim inside.

There are more possibilities too. Sheetweb spiders weave flat webs that stretch across bushes or grassy fields. There are even spiders that make small silk nets. They toss their nets over prey to catch dinner.

How the Other Half Lives

Only about half of the world's spiders spin webs. How does the other half catch dinner? Lots of ways!

Trap-door spiders, for example, live in holes. They make doors out of silk and dirt. At night a spider raises the door and sticks its head out. It grabs anything edible that walks by.

Jumping spiders sneak up on tasty-looking animals, then pounce on them.

Hairy Legs. *This fuzzy beast (left) is a tarantula. Tarantulas hunt other creatures, including mice, frogs, birds, and snakes.*

Wolf spiders, crab spiders, and tarantulas also hunt other critters.

Once the prey is dead, spiders use their jaws to make their favorite recipe: mashed meat with digestive juices. Spiders aren't picky eaters. Bees, flies, moths—they're all good. Tarantulas even eat mice and small birds.

Handy Appetites

All that eating adds up. **Arachnologists**, scientists who study spiders, are always exploring ways to learn just how much spiders actually eat.

One research team, for example, studied spiders living on an acre of farmland. Added together, spiders there ate about 75 pounds of insects each day. That's roughly like eating 750 hot dogs!

Without spiders' big appetites, the balance of life on Earth would be awfully different. We'd be sharing the planet with lots more insects.

And don't forget all that spider venom that Chuck Kristensen collects. It could become a key ingredient in germ-busting medicines.

You may never *like* spiders. You probably wouldn't ever want 50,000 of them in your home. But honestly, aren't you glad that spiders are in your world?

Wordwise

abdomen: back half of a spider's body
arachnid: spider or related animal
arachnologist: scientist who studies arachnids
prey: animals eaten by other animals
venom: poison

A Class Act

Look at the animals on these two pages. What do you notice about them? What creepy similarities do you see?

For starters, the animals all race around on eight legs. They all have a hard body covering. These critters all live on land. And they all look just a little bit alike.

These three animals have quite a lot in common. In fact, they are related. Scientists say that spiders, ticks, and scorpions belong to the same class. In this case, the word *class* doesn't mean a school class. It means these animals are part of a group with many similarities.

Getting Into Groups

Scientists sort living things into groups. It helps them know who or what is related—and how. It helps them make sense of the natural world.

Scientists start by thinking big. They divide living things into five basic categories called kingdoms. So, for example, all plants belong to one kingdom. All animals belong to another.

Do you know what that means? You're related to spiders! You're both animals. You both belong to the animal kingdom.

Scorpion

Tick

Differences Divide

You are in the same kingdom as spiders. But that's where the similarity stops.

You see, a kingdom is divided into phyla. A phylum is split into classes. A class is split into orders, and so on down to species. The more groups you share with something, the more alike you are.

Spiders and people share only one group. That's because we don't have much in common with spiders. Our bodies are very different. For example, you have a skeleton inside your body. Spiders wear their skeletons on the outside instead.

Striking Similarities

Spiders, ticks, and scorpions are much more closely related. They share the same kingdom, phylum, and class.

That means they show some striking similarities. Members of the Arachnida class have a hard covering. Most have two main body sections and eight legs. They breathe air, and they don't like to swim.

Arachnids include ticks, mites, spiders, scorpions, and a few other critters. Worldwide, there are more than 60,000 different members of the Arachnida class.

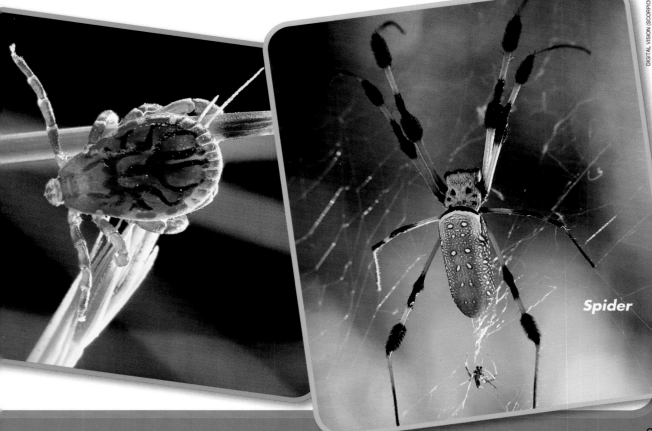

Spider

DIGITAL VISION (SCORPION); DARLENE A. MURAWSKI (TICK); DIGITAL VISION (SPIDER).

Which Is It?

How do you know whether an animal is a spider or an insect? Do what scientists do. Study its body. Look at these animals. Then answer the questions.

1 How many legs does each animal have? Hint: Some things that look like legs might not be.

2 How many body sections does each animal have? What does this tell you about the animal?

3 Which animals are arachnids? Which are insects? How did you decide which is which?

DIGITAL VISION (ORANGE INSECT); PHOTODISC (OTHERS)

Spiders

Take a spin at answering these questions about spiders.

1 What do you call a scientist who studies spiders?

2 What are some of the ways a spider catches its prey?

3 What are some of the characteristics of animals in the Arachnida class?

4 How is a spider's silk important even if the spider doesn't make webs?

5 Why might farmers be glad that spiders live in and around their crops?

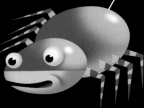